Essential

CARIBBEAN

Essential
CARIBBEAN

HAMLYN

First published in Great Britain in 1997 by Hamlyn
an imprint of Octopus Publishing Group Limited
2-4 Heron Quays London E14 4JP
Reprinted in 1999

Designed and produced by SP Creative Design

Editor and writer: Heather Thomas
Art director: Al Rockall
Designer: Rolando Ugolini

ISBN 0 600 59355 X

A CIP catalogue record for this book is available from the
British Library.

Printed in China

Acknowledgements
Special photography: Steve Baxter
Step-by-step photography: GGS Photographics, Norwich
Food preparation: Meg Jansz and Caroline Stevens

Notes
1. Standard spoon measurements are used in all recipes.
1 tablespoon = one 15ml spoon
1 teaspoon = one 5ml spoon

2. Both imperial and metric measurements have been
given in all recipes. Use one set of measurements only
and not a mixture of both.

3. Eggs should be medium unless otherwise stated.

4. Milk should be full fat unless otherwise stated.

5. Fresh herbs should be used unless otherwise stated.
If unavailable, use dried herbs as an alternative, but halve
the quantities stated.

CONTENTS

INTRODUCTION

There are over 200 islands in the thin chain that stretches for 2,600 miles from Florida in the north to Venezuela in the south. To the east of these islands lie the turbulent waters of the Atlantic Ocean, whereas to the west they are lapped by the calmer, clear waters of the warm Caribbean Sea. The islands are still a fascinating melting pot of different people, each with their own traditions, culture and culinary heritage.

The food they eat, its preparation and presentation, reflects the diversity of their origins. Many dishes can be traced back to the cooking of the Caribs and Arawaks, the islands' original inhabitants, as well as to the British, Spanish, Dutch, French and, of course, the Africans who brought their own ingredients and cooking skills when they were transported to the islands to work on the vast new sugar plantations. In the nineteenth century, Indian and Chinese immigrants arrived in Trinidad, bringing with them a love of hot, spicy food, curries and rice dishes, and these too have now become an intrinsic part of Caribbean cooking.

Exotic fruits, tropical vegetables, spices and seafood are abundant, and all contribute to the unique cuisine of the islands. Most savoury dishes are highly seasoned with freshly picked spices, hot pepper sauces, garlic and coconut. If you visit the markets in the small towns, you will see piles of huge golden pumpkins, bundles of hot chillies, fibrous coconuts, gigantic dark green callaloo leaves, fists of black plantains, and the ubiquitous yams, sweet potatoes, cassava, breadfruit, okra and christophenes, alongside clay cooking pots and local basketware.

The old women have an enticing array of spices for sale: fresh nutmegs in their delicate filigree of crimson mace, bundles of aromatic cinnamon bark, little bags of allspice berries, cloves and black peppercorns, and crumbling cocoa sticks. To experience the real atmosphere of the Caribbean and to sample the native foods, you must visit one of these colourful, bustling markets or eat at one of the many roadside stands or family-run rum shacks. This is where the best and most authentic Caribbean food is usually to be discovered, far away from the tourist beaches and hotels.

Allspice

These dark brown berries resemble black peppercorns and come from an evergreen tree in the bay family. Sometimes known as pimento or Jamaica pepper, they can be used whole or ground. They have a very distinctive flavour, which is reminiscent of cinnamon, cloves, juniper berries and nutmeg. Allspice berries are particularly popular in Jamaica, where 'jerked' meat and chicken are often grilled over allspice branches to impart more flavour to the finished dish.

Bananas

There are many varieties of banana in the Caribbean, ranging from small red and yellow-skinned ones to the large black plantains. Green bananas may be cooked and served as a savoury dish, whereas

yellow ones may be eaten as a snack or dessert. Thus bananas are boiled, fried, curried, grilled, baked and stuffed. You will find recipes for many of these dishes in this book. Banana leaves also have their uses and make a good substitute for foil when wrapping and cooking food.

Callaloo

These are the gigantic green spreading leaves of the dasheen, eddo or taro plant, which grows in the tropical rainforests of the Caribbean. When cooked, they resemble spinach, and have given their name to the islands' most famous soup.

Chillies

There are many different varieties of chillies, all with exotic names like bird peppers and Scotch bonnets. They originated in Mexico and were brought to the Caribbean by the Spanish. The hottest chillies of all are the Scotch bonnets, beloved of the Jamaicans, and these are pale green, red or yellow. They are added to many dishes, immersed in oils, or crushed with vinegar and made into the hot sauces which appear on every Caribbean dinner table.

Christophenes

This pale green, pear-shaped vegetable is also known as chayote or cho-cho. It has a delicate flavour, which is similar to that of marrow, and a distinctively crisp texture. In the Caribbean, it is served

baked, stuffed, boiled or even dressed in salads. Christophenes are usually boiled in their skins, although they may be peeled before cooking.

Cinnamon

These scented bark quills come from the inner bark of the cinnamon tree, which grows widely in Grenada and some of the other islands. In the Caribbean, cinnamon is always sold in its bark form, tied into rough bundles, and then it can be ground into powder as required.

Cloves

These are actually unopened flower buds, and they may be purchased either whole or ground. For maximum strength and aroma, it is always best to grind them yourself before adding to a dish.

Coconuts

The coconut has so many culinary and practical uses in the Caribbean. It may be split open and the coconut water consumed as a refreshing drink; or the water may be mixed with the grated flesh to make coconut milk. This is added to many classic savoury and sweet dishes. The coconut flesh is also used in cooking, while the fibrous outer coating of the coconut is used for weaving floor and wall coverings.

Conch

Most people are more familiar with the beautiful pearly pink shell of this mollusc than the meat inside. It is considered a great delicacy throughout the Caribbean, and is thought to be an aphrodisiac. Indeed, young men are encouraged to eat conch to improve their virility. Before cooking, conch (pronounced 'conk') is beaten to tenderize it. Likewise, it is important to avoid over-cooking or it may be very rubbery and tough. It is difficult to obtain fresh conch outside of the Caribbean, although it can be bought in cans in many West Indian specialist shops.

Coriander

This pungent herb is used extensively in the Spanish-speaking islands of the Caribbean. The leaves are used for garnishing and flavouring savoury dishes, whereas the seeds are ground as a spice.

Limes

It is hard to imagine Caribbean food without limes. They are used in so many dishes, both sweet and savoury, as well as in drinks and punches. Limes are a tropical citrus fruit and cannot be grown successfully in more temperate and Mediterranean climates. When buying limes, always choose fresh, plump ones, and avoid any wrinkled or dry-looking fruit. Limes complement many chicken and fish dishes; often the juice is added to marinades, sauces and basting mixtures.

Molasses

These are a by-product of refining sugar cane. Dark brown, almost black, in colour, they have long been used in the West Indies as a natural sweetening agent. With their subtly spicy flavour, they have a natural affinity with bananas and many other exotic fruits.

Nutmeg

Nutmeg and mace are widely used spices which both come from the same tree. The aromatic nutmeg is encapsulated in a tough dark outer casing which, in turn, is wrapped in a filigree of crimson mace. As it ages, the mace fades from bright red to a dull golden colour. Nutmeg is always at its most pungent when grated fresh rather than using the ground powder. In the Caribbean it is used for flavouring soups, curries, desserts and drinks.

Okra

This pale green, spear-shaped vegetable was imported from Africa and is now an essential ingredient in many Caribbean dishes. It is added to many soups, stews, sauces and curries and has a thickening quality. However, it also tends to be rather slimey and sticky in texture when cooked. You can combat the worst of the stickiness by washing and drying the okra pods before cooking. Okra is also known as ladyfingers or gumbo.

Pepper sauces

No West Indian table would be complete without the requisite bottle of hot pepper sauce, and every island has its own speciality. These sauces range from fiery reds through shades of orange to golds and yellows. They are used as a seasoning for most dishes, but do take care when using them as they can be incredibly hot!

Plantains

These resemble large bananas, and when unripe (green) or semi-ripe (yellow) they are cooked as a starchy vegetable or added to stews and savoury dishes. Their skin turns black as they ripen and they may then be used in desserts. Plantains are never eaten raw; they are always cooked.

Rum

The distilled spirit of sugar cane or molasses is used in West Indian cooking as well as drinks, especially rum punch and planter's punch. Rums vary considerably in flavour and quality, and while some are very rough and unrefined, others are on a par with the finest French brandies. Each island has its own specialities.

Saltfish

Salted cod was originally the staple food of slaves working on the plantations, but it is now considered a delicacy and has become Jamaica's national dish. It should always be washed thoroughly and soaked overnight in several changes of water before using.

Sweet potatoes

These starchy vegetables are eaten widely throughout the islands, and are used in both sweet and savoury dishes. The flesh may be orange, yellow or white, while the skins are red or orange. Always buy whole, uncut sweet potatoes and handle them very gently. They can be boiled or baked in their skins, or they may be mashed like ordinary potatoes.

Yams

These edible tubers are similar to potatoes, but have a nuttier flavour. Yams originated in Africa and were brought to the West Indies by the African slaves. Despite their unprepossessing appearance, they are revered by West Indian cooks and may be boiled, grilled or barbecued.

Cooking utensils

Traditional Caribbean cooking utensils are rustic and practical. They can be bought in local markets alongside the fruit and vegetables on display. However, all the dishes in this book can be cooked with conventional modern Western cookware if you cannot obtain the authentic pots and dishes.

Canarees: these are earthenware casserole and pie dishes.

Coalpots: these are traditional iron or clay pots which are perfect for slow-cooked dishes, such as pepperpots.

Pestle and mortar: large or small, these are commonly used for grinding spices and pounding foods.

Yabbas: these glazed clay pots have many practical uses, e.g. storage, mixing and cooking.

SOUPE GERMOU

Pumpkin soup (St Lucia)

50g/2oz butter
2 onions, finely chopped
1 garlic clove, chopped
1kg/2lb wedge of pumpkin
1 large tomato, skinned, seeded and chopped
2 sprigs of parsley
1 bay leaf
1.2 litres/2 pints chicken stock
pinch of sugar
salt and freshly ground black pepper
200ml/7 fl oz single cream
dash of hot pepper sauce

For the garnish:

chopped chives
grated fresh nutmeg

1 Melt the butter in a large saucepan over low heat. Add the onions and garlic and stir well. Cook slowly in the butter until the onions are soft and golden, but take care that they do not brown.

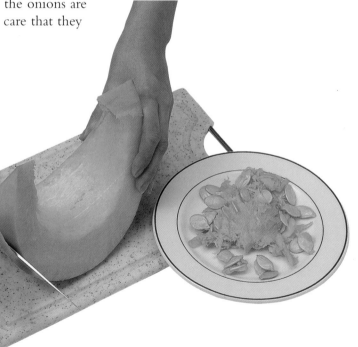

2 While the onions are cooking, remove the rind, seeds and any stringy bits from the pumpkin and cut the flesh into small chunks. Add to the onions in the pan with the tomato and herbs, and sauté for 2-3 minutes.

3 Add the chicken stock, sugar and seasoning. Cover the pan and simmer gently over low heat for 30-40 minutes, until the pumpkin starts to break up into the soup. Remove the parsley and bay leaf and then purée the soup in a food processor or blender until smooth.

4 Return the puréed soup to the pan and stir in the cream and hot pepper sauce. Check the seasoning and then heat through gently. Serve in bowls garnished with chives and grated nutmeg.

PREPARATION: 10 MINUTES
COOKING: 45-55 MINUTES
SERVES: 6

CALLALOO
Barbados

1 Wash the callaloo or spinach leaves thoroughly under running cold water to remove any dirt. Drain, shake dry and then roughly chop them, cutting out and discarding any hard stems.

2 Heat the groundnut oil in a large saucepan and add the onion, spring onions and garlic. Fry gently for 5 minutes, or until softened. Add the red chilli, turmeric and thyme, and stir over low heat for 1-2 minutes.

PREPARATION: 15 MINUTES
COOKING: 35 MINUTES
SERVES: 6

3 Stir in the okra and then add the chopped callaloo or spinach leaves. Turn up the heat and cook, stirring, until the leaves start to wilt. Reduce the heat and add the chicken stock and saffron. Bring to the boil, and then cover and simmer for 20 minutes.

500g/1lb fresh callaloo or spinach leaves
3 tablespoons groundnut oil
1 large onion, finely chopped
4 spring onions, chopped
2 garlic cloves, crushed
1 fresh red chilli, seeded and finely chopped
1 teaspoon turmeric
sprig of thyme, crumbled
250g/8oz okra, sliced thinly
900ml/1½ pints chicken stock
few strands of saffron
425ml/14 fl oz coconut milk
250g/8oz crab meat, fresh or canned
salt and freshly ground black pepper
juice of ½ lime
dash of hot pepper sauce

4 Add the coconut milk and crab meat and stir well. Heat gently for 4-5 minutes and then season to taste with salt and pepper. Just before serving, stir in the lime juice and hot pepper sauce.

PEPPERPOT SOUP

Jamaica

| 1kg/2lb lean stewing beef |
| 250g/8oz lean pork |
| 1.8 litres/3 pints water |
| 500g/1lb kale, chopped |
| 500g/1lb callaloo or spinach leaves, washed and chopped |
| 1 onion, chopped |
| 2 green peppers, seeded and chopped |
| 2 spring onions, chopped |
| 250g/8oz yam, peeled and sliced |
| 1 large potato, sliced |
| 1 sprig of thyme |
| 1 garlic clove, crushed |
| 24 okras, trimmed and sliced |
| 25g/1oz butter |
| 150ml/¼ pint coconut milk |
| salt and freshly ground black pepper |

For the 'dumplins':

| 250g/8oz flour |
| pinch of salt |
| 2 teaspoons baking powder |
| 25g/1oz margarine |

1 Trim any fat from the beef and pork and cut the meat into cubes. Place in a large saucepan with the water and bring to the boil. Reduce the heat, cover the pan and simmer gently for 45 minutes.

3 While the soup is cooking, make the 'dumplins'. Sift the flour, salt and baking powder into a bowl and rub in the margarine. Add sufficient water to mix to a stiff dough. Knead until soft and smooth and shape into 18 balls. Flatten them and cook in salted boiling water for 10 minutes.

2 Add the kale, callaloo or spinach leaves, onion, green peppers, spring onions, yam, potato, thyme and garlic. Simmer gently in the covered pan for 15-30 minutes, until the vegetables are tender and the meat is cooked.

PREPARATION: 30 MINUTES
COOKING: 1¼ HOURS
SERVES: 6

4 In a frying pan, fry the okra in the butter until golden brown on both sides. Remove and drain. Add to the soup with the coconut milk and simmer for 5 minutes. Season to taste and serve in individual bowls with the hot 'dumplins'.

FISH SOUP

Guadeloupe

1 Put the fish heads, bones and trimmings in a large saucepan with the water. Shell the prawns, and add the heads, tails and shells to the fish trimmings in the pan with the black peppercorns and bay leaf. Reserve the shelled prawns.

2 Place the pan over high heat and bring to the boil. Reduce the heat and cover the pan, and then simmer gently for 30 minutes. Strain the fish stock through a sieve into a large bowl and set aside.

3 Heat the oil in a large saucepan and add the onion, garlic and green pepper. Sauté until the onion is softened and golden. Add the spring onions and tomatoes and continue cooking for 2 minutes, stirring.

500g/1lb filleted white fish, e.g. bass, bream, plus heads, bones and trimmings
1.8 litres/3 pints water
250g/8oz cooked prawns
4 whole black peppercorns
1 bay leaf
3 tablespoons oil
1 large onion, chopped
2 garlic cloves, crushed
1 small green pepper, seeded and chopped
3 spring onions, chopped
3 tomatoes, skinned, seeded and chopped
1/4 teaspoon saffron powder
strip of lime peel
2 cloves
2 allspice berries
salt and freshly ground black pepper
dash of lime juice

PREPARATION: 15 MINUTES
COOKING: 1 HOUR 10 MINUTES
SERVES: 6

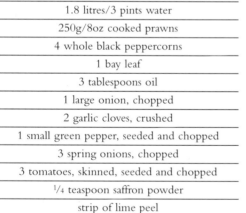

4 Add the reserved fish stock, saffron, lime peel, cloves and allspice berries. Bring to the boil and then reduce the heat and simmer for 15 minutes. Add the white fish fillets and prawns and cook gently for 10 minutes. Season to taste and add a dash of lime juice. Serve hot.

CHILLED AVOCADO SOUP
Bahamas

3 Cut the avocados in half and remove the thick green rind and stones. Place the flesh in a bowl and mash well with a fork. Add the crab meat and mix thoroughly together.

1 Melt the butter in a large saucepan over low heat. Add the onion and garlic and stir well. Cook gently, without colouring, until the onion is soft and translucent.

50g/2oz butter
1 onion, finely chopped
1 garlic clove, crushed
1 tablespoon flour
1.2 litres/2 pints chicken stock
4 ripe avocados
250g/8oz crab meat, fresh or canned
300ml/½ pint single cream
salt and freshly ground black pepper
To garnish:
sliced avocado
chopped chives or coriander

2 Stir in the flour and cook gently, stirring continuously, for 1-2 minutes. Do not allow the flour to brown. Add the chicken stock, a little at a time, and continue stirring until the flour is mixed in thoroughly and the liquid is smooth and free from lumps. Bring to the boil and then reduce the heat.

PREPARATION: 10 MINUTES +
CHILLING TIME
COOKING: 30-35 MINUTES
SERVES: 6

4 Add the mashed avocado and crab meat to the soup and simmer gently for 15-20 minutes. Stir in the cream and season to taste with salt and pepper. Remove from the heat and set aside to cool. Cover and chill in the refrigerator. Serve chilled, garnished with sliced avocado and chives or coriander.

ACRATS DE MORUE
Salt-codfish fritters (Guadeloupe)

1 Make the batter: sift the flour into a bowl. Beat the eggs with the melted butter and then add to the flour. Beat well and then gradually beat in the milk, a little at a time. If the batter is too stiff, thin it down with a little more milk. Cover and set aside for 2-3 hours.

2 Put the salt-codfish in a bowl and cover with warm water. Set aside to soak for 2-3 hours. During this time, you should change the water at least twice. Drain the fish well, and then remove the skin and bones.

175g/6oz plain flour
2 eggs
40g/1½oz butter, melted and cooled
250ml/8 fl oz milk
250g/8oz salt-codfish
1 fresh red chilli, seeded and finely chopped
2 spring onions, finely chopped
1 garlic clove, crushed
1 tablespoon chopped parsley
½ teaspoon dried thyme
salt and freshly ground black pepper
oil for deep-frying
hot pepper sauce, to serve

PREPARATION: 15 MINUTES +
STANDING + SOAKING TIME
COOKING: 5-10 MINUTES
SERVES: 6

3 Flake the fish and place in a mortar with the chilli, spring onions, garlic, herbs and seasoning. Pound until smooth. Alternatively, purée in a blender or food processor. Mix into the batter and leave to stand for 30 minutes.

4 Heat the oil in a deep-fryer or heavy saucepan to 190°C/375°F. Drop spoonfuls of the fish mixture into the oil and fry in batches until golden all over. Remove with a perforated spoon and drain on absorbent kitchen paper. Serve hot with hot pepper sauce.

HONEYED CHICKEN WINGS

Grenadines

3 tablespoons soy sauce

4 tablespoons runny honey

2 tablespoons vinegar

1 tablespoon sherry

2 teaspoons soft brown sugar

1/2 teaspoon ground ginger

1 garlic clove, crushed

12 chicken wings, trimmed

For the dipping sauce:

2 tablespoons grated onion

2 tablespoons olive oil

2 tablespoons brown sugar

1 teaspoon lime juice

2 tablespoons peanut butter

6 tablespoons coconut cream

pinch of salt

2 Put the chicken wings in a shallow bowl and pour the honey marinade over the top. Smear the marinade all over the wings, then cover and leave in a cool place to marinate for 2 hours.

1 Put the soy sauce, honey, vinegar, sherry, sugar, ginger and garlic in a bowl and mix well together, blending thoroughly until smooth.

PREPARATION: 15 MINUTES +
MARINATING TIME
COOKING: 15-20 MINUTES
SERVES: 4

3 While the wings are marinating, make the sauce. Fry the onion in the oil for about 5 minutes until golden brown. Stir in the sugar, lime juice and peanut butter, and then add the coconut cream, a little at a time. Add the salt and cook over gentle heat until smooth and thick. Set aside.

4 Remove the chicken wings from the marinade and place on a rack in a baking pan. Cook in a preheated oven at 190°C/375°F/Gas Mark 5 for 15-20 minutes, until crisp and golden brown and cooked through. Baste from time to time with any leftover marinade. Alternatively, grill for 5-7 minutes each side. Serve with the warm peanut dipping sauce.

RUN DOWN

Jamaica

500g/1lb mackerel or other small fish
juice of 1 lime
900ml/1½ pints coconut milk
1 onion, grated
1 garlic clove, crushed
2 green peppers, seeded and chopped
1 fresh red chilli, seeded and finely chopped
3 tomatoes, skinned and chopped
2 teaspoons chopped thyme
2 teaspoons chopped chives
1 tablespoon malt vinegar
salt and freshly ground black pepper

1 Clean and scale the mackerel and then remove the bones and fillet them. Put them in a bowl and pour the lime juice over the top. Set aside in a cool place.

4 Add the marinated mackerel fillets and lime juice, and continue cooking gently until the fish is cooked and tender. Serve with fried bananas as a first course.

2 Pour the coconut milk into a deep, heavy-based frying pan. Bring the coconut milk to the boil and continue boiling for about 15 minutes, until it becomes oily.

PREPARATION: 15 MINUTES
COOKING: 35 MINUTES
SERVES: 4

3 Add the onion, garlic, green peppers and chilli and cook gently for about 5 minutes, until the onion is softened but not brown. Add the tomatoes, thyme, chives and vinegar and stir well. Cook gently over low heat for 10 minutes. Season to taste.

ROTI

Curried pancake snacks (Trinidad)

250g/8oz plain flour

¹/₂ teaspoon bicarbonate of soda

pinch of salt

4–5 tablespoons milk

ghee for frying

For the filling:

Colombo de Porc (see page 58) or
Curried Prawns (see page 44)

1 Sift the flour, bicarbonate of soda and salt into a bowl. Bind together with enough milk to form a stiff dough. Knead lightly with your hands and transfer to a lightly floured surface.

3 Heat a griddle and cook the roti until lightly browned on both sides, turning them frequently during cooking. Keep brushing them with a little ghee to prevent them sticking.

PREPARATION: 10 MINUTES +
STANDING TIME
COOKING: 10 MINUTES
MAKES: 8

2 With floured hands, divide the dough into 8 pieces and then roll into balls, about the size of an egg. Flatten them out and spread with a little ghee, and then pat back to an egg shape again before flattening them once more. Leave to stand for 30 minutes.

4 Remove the roti from the griddle and place in the palm of one hand. Clap your hands together around the roti several times. You can use a cloth to prevent burning your hands. Fill the roti with Colombo de Porc or Curried Prawns and roll up.

ESCOVITCH

Pickled fish (Jamaica)

2 In the oil remaining in the pan, fry the white fish fillets until they are lightly browned on both sides, turning once. Lift out the fillets and arrange them in a large serving dish. Place the onions and peppers on top of the fish.

1 Heat 4 tablespoons of the oil in a large, heavy frying pan and add the onions and peppers. Fry over gentle heat until the onions are tender and golden and the peppers are soft. Remove with a perforated spoon and set aside.

6 tablespoons olive oil
2 onions, thinly sliced
2 green peppers, seeded and sliced
1kg/2lb white fish fillets
450ml/³/₄ pint water
1 bay leaf
2.5cm/1-inch piece fresh root ginger, peeled and chopped
6 peppercorns
¹/₈ teaspoon mace
salt and freshly ground black pepper
150ml/¹/₄ pint malt vinegar
For the garnish:
black olives
sweet red pimientos

PREPARATION: 10 MINUTES
COOKING: 25-30 MINUTES
SERVES: 8 (AS A FIRST COURSE)

3 Put the water in a saucepan with the bay leaf, ginger, peppercorns and mace. Season with salt and pepper and simmer gently for 15 minutes. Add the remaining olive oil and the vinegar and simmer for 2 more minutes.

4 Strain the liquid and discard the bay leaf and spices. Pour the strained liquid over the fish fillets, onions and peppers. This dish can either be served hot, or it can be cooled and then chilled before serving cold. Garnish with black olives and pimientos.

DAUBE DE POISSONS

Tuna in tomato sauce (Martinique)

1 Put the tuna steaks in a shallow dish. Blend together the lime juice, garlic, chilli and salt, and sprinkle over the tuna steaks. Pour the water over the top and leave to marinate in a cool place for 1–2 hours.

2 Drain the tuna and throw away the marinade. Dredge the tuna with flour and then fry in the oil in a large frying pan until golden brown on both sides. Remove from the pan and keep warm while you make the sauce.

3 Add the onion, spring onions and red pepper to the oil in the frying pan and fry gently until softened. Stir in the tomatoes and add the bay leaf, thyme, seasoning and wine or water. Simmer gently for a few minutes.

| 4 tuna steaks |
| juice of 2 limes |
| 2 garlic cloves, crushed |
| 1 fresh red chilli, seeded and crushed |
| pinch of salt |
| 300ml/½ pint water |
| flour for dredging |
| 3 tablespoons olive oil |
| 1 onion, finely chopped |
| 3 spring onions, chopped |
| 1 red pepper, seeded and chopped |
| 3 tomatoes, skinned and chopped |
| 1 bay leaf |
| sprig of fresh thyme |
| salt and freshly ground black pepper |
| 50ml/2 fl oz dry white wine or water |
| **To serve:** |
| juice of ½ lime |
| 1 tablespoon olive oil |
| lime wedges |

4 Add the tuna steaks to the tomato sauce in the pan. Cover and continue cooking gently for 10 minutes, or until the tuna is cooked. Stir in the lime juice and olive oil, and serve immediately with a garnish of lime wedges.

PREPARATION: 10 MINUTES
+ MARINATING TIME
COOKING: 25 MINUTES
SERVES: 4

SPICY BAKED FISH

Windward Islands

| 1 x 1.5-2kg/3-4lb sea bass (or bream), cleaned and scaled |
| juice of 2 limes |
| salt and freshly ground black pepper |
| 1 onion, thinly sliced |
| 6 tablespoons olive oil |
| fresh coriander, to garnish |

For the stuffing:

| 125g/4oz soft breadcrumbs |
| 50g/2oz butter, melted |
| 1 tablespoon finely chopped chives |
| 1 teaspoon finely chopped coriander |
| 1 small green pepper, seeded and finely chopped |
| 1/2 onion, grated |
| grated rind and juice of 1 lime |
| pinch of grated nutmeg |
| salt and freshly ground black pepper |

For the topping:

| 2 tablespoons oil |
| 1 small onion, chopped |
| 1 garlic clove, crushed |
| 1 fresh red chilli, seeded and chopped |
| 1 tablespoon chopped coriander |
| 4 tablespoons fish stock |

1 Make the stuffing: put the breadcrumbs in a bowl and mix in the melted butter and all the remaining ingredients. Blend well and then set aside to cool.

2 Wash and dry the fish and place in a large dish. Sprinkle it with the lime juice and season inside and out. Set aside in a cool place for about 1 hour to marinate.

PREPARATION: 25 MINUTES
+ MARINATING TIME
COOKING: 30-40 MINUTES
SERVES: 4

3 Make the topping: heat the oil in a frying pan and add the onion and garlic. Fry gently until the onion is softened and golden. Add the chilli and continue cooking for 2-3 minutes. Stir in the coriander and fish stock.

4 Remove the fish from the marinade and fill it with the stuffing. Secure with skewers or toothpicks. Arrange the sliced onion in a large ovenproof dish and place the fish on top. Pour over the oil and any remaining marinade, and scatter the topping mixture over the fish. Bake in a preheated oven at 180°C/350°F/Gas Mark 4 for 30-40 minutes. Serve garnished with coriander.

POISSON EN BLAFF

Creole poached fish (Guadeloupe)

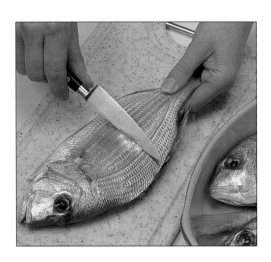

1 Wash, clean and scale the red snappers, leaving the heads and tails on. Pat dry with absorbent kitchen paper and place the fish in a shallow bowl.

2 Make the marinade: mix together the lime juice, crushed allspice and garlic with the seasoning and chopped chilli. Pour over the fish and leave to marinate in a cool place for 1 hour.

PREPARATION: 10 MINUTES +
MARINATING TIME
COOKING: 10-15 MINUTES
SERVES: 4

3 Put the water, wine, onion, spring onions and garlic in a large saucepan. Make a bouquet garni with the thyme, bay leaf, parsley and chives and tie together in a small bundle. Prick the chilli all over with a fork, and add to the pan with the bouquet garni and allspice berries.

4 small red snappers
600ml/1 pint water
150ml/¼ pint dry white wine
1 small onion, sliced
3 spring onions, chopped
1 garlic clove, peeled
1 sprig of fresh thyme
1 bay leaf
1 sprig of parsley
a few chives
1 fresh red chilli
2 allspice berries
boiled rice and fried bananas, to serve
For the marinade:
juice of 4 limes
2 allspice berries, crushed
2 garlic cloves, crushed
salt and freshly ground black pepper
1 fresh red chilli, seeded and finely chopped

4 Bring to the boil and then add the marinated fish. When the liquid returns to the boil, reduce the heat and simmer for 5-10 minutes, until cooked. Discard the bouquet garni. Remove the fish and serve in bowls with the poaching liquid ladled over the top. Serve with rice and fried bananas.

FISH WITH HOT PEPPER SAUCE

St Lucia

1 Make the hot pepper sauce: heat the groundnut oil in a saucepan and add the onions and garlic. Fry over medium heat until softened and golden brown. Add the chillies and allspice berries, and continue cooking for 3-4 minutes. Set aside to cool a little.

2 Put the onion and spice mixture in a blender or food processor and process for 1 minute. Remove and then blend in the seasoning, lime juice and vinegar.

4 Heat the oil in a large frying pan and add the tuna steaks. Fry on both sides until cooked and golden brown. Remove and drain on absorbent kitchen paper and then serve with the hot pepper sauce. Take care not to use too much sauce as it is very hot. Leftover sauce can be stored for a few days in the refrigerator.

3 Place the tuna steaks in a bowl and pour over the lime juice and a little salt, rubbing it in well. Dredge them with flour and then dip them first into the beaten egg and then into the breadcrumbs, coating them well.

PREPARATION: 20 MINUTES
COOKING: 15 MINUTES
SERVES: 4

4 thick fish steaks, e.g. tuna
juice of 2 limes
salt
flour for dredging
1 egg, beaten
breadcrumbs for coating
oil for shallow-frying
For the hot pepper sauce:
2 tablespoons groundnut oil
2 onions, finely chopped
2 garlic cloves, chopped
12 fresh red chillies, seeded and finely chopped
2 allspice berries, crushed
salt and freshly ground black pepper
juice of 1 lime
75ml/3 fl oz malt vinegar

FISH CURRY

Barbados

40g/1½oz butter

1 large onion, finely chopped

1 garlic clove, crushed

1 tablespoon curry powder

1 tablespoon flour

400ml/14 fl oz coconut milk

½ fresh green chilli, seeded and chopped

625g/1¼lb white fish fillets

juice of ½ lime

salt and freshly ground black pepper

chopped coriander, to garnish

boiled rice and mango chutney, to serve

1 Melt the butter in a heavy-based frying pan over low heat, taking care that it does not brown. Add the onion and garlic and cook gently until softened and golden.

3 While the curry sauce is cooking, skin the white fish fillets with a sharp knife. Discard the skin and arrange the fillets in a shallow ovenproof dish. Squeeze the lime juice over the top.

2 Add the curry powder and flour and stir well. Cook gently over very low heat for 2 minutes, stirring. Add the coconut milk and chilli, and stir well to mix them thoroughly. Simmer gently over low heat for 5-10 minutes until smooth and thickened.

4 Season the curry sauce and pour over the fish fillets. Cover the dish and cook in a preheated oven at 170°C/325°F/Gas Mark 3 for 12-15 minutes, until the fish is just cooked but still firm. Serve, sprinkled with coriander, with boiled rice and mango chutney.

PREPARATION: 10 MINUTES
COOKING: 25-30 MINUTES
SERVES: 4

CURRIED SHRIMP PILAU
Tobago

500g/1lb uncooked large prawns

juice of 2 limes

4 tablespoons groundnut oil

1 large onion, chopped

2 garlic cloves, crushed

1 fresh red chilli, seeded and finely chopped

1 green pepper, seeded and chopped

2-3 teaspoons curry powder

375g/12oz long-grain rice

650ml/1¼ pints coconut milk

salt and freshly ground black pepper

For the garnish:

chopped coriander

whole cooked prawns and fresh red chillies

1 Shell the prawns, removing the heads, shells, legs and tails. Take out the black intestinal vein running along the back. Put the shelled prawns in a bowl and sprinkle the lime juice over the top. Set aside to marinate while you make the pilau.

3 Add the rice and stir well until all the grains are glistening with oil. Pour in the coconut milk and mix well. Cover the pan and cook over very low heat for 15-20 minutes, until the rice is tender and all the liquid has been absorbed. Check the rice occasionally, stirring to prevent it sticking. Add more liquid if necessary.

4 Add the prawns and their lime juice marinade to the rice, stirring through to distribute them evenly. Season to taste with salt and pepper, and heat through gently. Serve hot garnished with coriander, prawns and chillies.

2 Heat the groundnut oil in a large, deep frying pan and add the onion, garlic, chilli and green pepper. Fry gently until the onion and pepper are softened but not brown. Stir in the curry powder and cook for 2-3 minutes.

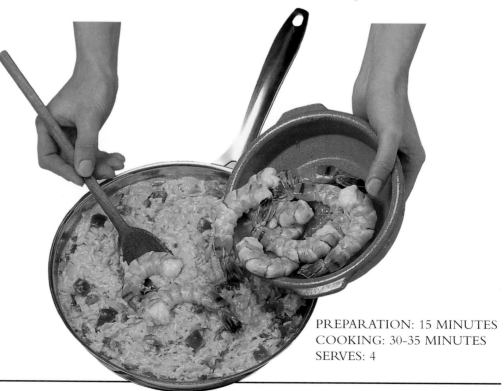

PREPARATION: 15 MINUTES
COOKING: 30-35 MINUTES
SERVES: 4

CRAB CREOLE

Martinique

1 Remove the crab claws and legs and crack them to extract the meat. Open the crabs by pressing with your thumbs on the edge of the section of the shell to which the legs were attached. Pull out the central section.

2 Discard the stomach sac and feathery gills. Scoop out the meat from inside the shell and put in a bowl with the meat from the claws and legs. Remove the meat from the leg sockets with a skewer and mix with the other crab meat. Mash well with a fork.

4 medium-sized cooked crabs
75g/3oz breadcrumbs
2 red peppers, seeded and finely chopped
1 garlic clove, crushed
1 fresh red chilli, seeded and finely chopped
pinch of ground mace
1/2 teaspoon ground allspice berries
2 tablespoons chopped parsley
juice of 1 lime
2 tablespoons rum (optional)
salt and freshly ground black pepper
15g/1/2oz butter

PREPARATION: 25 MINUTES
COOKING: 30 MINUTES
SERVES: 4

3 Add 50g/2oz of the breadcrumbs to the crab meat, together with the red peppers, garlic, chilli, mace, allspice and parsley. Add the lime juice and rum (if using) and season with salt and pepper.

4 Scrub and wash the empty crab shells and fill with the crab meat stuffing mixture. Sprinkle with the remaining breadcrumbs and dot with butter. Bake in a preheated oven at 180°C/350°F/Gas Mark 4 for 30 minutes, until browned.

CURRIED PRAWNS IN PINEAPPLE

Trinidad

750g/1½lb uncooked prawns
juice of 1 lime
2 tablespoons vegetable oil
1 onion, finely chopped
1 tablespoon chopped chives
2 tomatoes, skinned and chopped
2 tablespoons curry powder
300ml/½ pint fish stock or water
25g/1oz butter, softened
25g/1oz flour
2 small pineapples
chopped chives, to garnish

1 Shell the prawns and remove the black intestinal vein running along the back of each prawn. Place the prawns in a bowl, sprinkle with the lime juice and set aside.

3 Add the fish stock or water and the prawns and stir well. Simmer over low heat for 15 minutes. Remove the pan from the heat. Blend the butter and flour together and add in small pieces to the prawn curry, stirring until thickened and smooth. Cook gently for 3 more minutes.

4 Plunge the pineapples into boiling water for 3 minutes and then drain. Cut them in half lengthways and hollow out some of the flesh. Spoon the curried prawn mixture into the hollowed-out pineapples and sprinkle with chives.

2 Heat the oil in a heavy frying pan and add the onion and chives. Cook gently for about 5 minutes until the onion is softened. Add the tomatoes and curry powder and continue cooking over low heat for about 5 minutes, stirring frequently.

PREPARATION: 15 MINUTES
COOKING: 30 MINUTES
SERVES: 4

PRAWNS WITH MANGO SAUCE

St Lucia

750g/1½lb uncooked king prawns

125g/4oz plain flour

pinch of salt

1 tablespoon olive oil

1 egg, separated

150ml/¼ pint coconut milk

oil for deep-frying

For the mango sauce:

4 large ripe mangoes

50ml/2 fl oz water

40g/1½oz caster sugar

pinch of ground ginger

pinch of ground cinnamon

1 teaspoon curry powder

juice of ½ lime

pinch of salt

3 Make the mango sauce: peel the mangoes and remove the stones. Cut up the flesh and process in a blender or food processor. Put the purée in a saucepan, add the water and stir over low heat until blended. Cover and simmer for 15-20 minutes until thickened. Stir in the sugar, spices, lime juice and salt and leave to cool down.

1 Remove the shells from the prawns, leaving the tails intact. Take out the black vein that runs along the back of each prawn and leave the prawns in a cool place while you make the batter and sauce.

2 Make the batter: put the flour, salt and olive oil in a bowl and make a well in the centre. Whisk the egg yolk with the coconut milk, and gradually add to the flour, beating well together. Cover and set aside.

4 Whisk the egg white until stiff and fold gently into the prepared batter. Add the prawns. Heat the oil for deep-frying to 190°C/375°F and fry the prawns, a few at a time, until golden brown. Remove and drain on absorbent kitchen paper. Serve immediately with the mango sauce.

PREPARATION: 15 MINUTES +
STANDING TIME
COOKING: 20-25 MINUTES
SERVES: 4

SEAFOOD CREOLE

Puerto Rico

1 Make the sofrito (a basic Puerto Rican tomato sauce). Heat the olive oil in a saucepan and add the onion and garlic. Fry over gentle heat until soft and translucent. Add the tomatoes and coriander, and season with salt and pepper. Simmer over very low heat for 20–30 minutes, until thickened.

2 In a large frying pan, sauté the onions, green peppers and garlic in the olive oil until softened and golden. Stir occasionally and do not allow them to brown.

3 Prepare the seafood, removing any shells from the lobster, prawns or crab meat. Add to the vegetables in the pan with the prepared sofrito. Simmer gently for 15 minutes.

| 2 onions, chopped |
| 2 green peppers, seeded and chopped |
| 2 garlic cloves, crushed |
| 4 tablespoons olive oil |
| 500g/1lb mixed seafood, e.g. cooked lobster meat, large prawns, crab meat |
| 4 tablespoons white wine |
| salt and freshly ground black pepper |
| sprigs of coriander, to garnish |
| boiled rice, to serve |

For the sofrito:

| 3 tablespoons olive oil |
| 1 onion, chopped |
| 3 garlic cloves, crushed |
| 500g/1lb tomatoes, skinned and chopped |
| 1 tablespoon chopped coriander |
| salt and freshly ground black pepper |

PREPARATION: 30 MINUTES
COOKING: 25 MINUTES
SERVES: 4

4 Add the wine and stir well. Continue cooking for 5 minutes. Adjust the seasoning and serve garnished with coriander, accompanied by plain boiled rice.

SPICY RED SNAPPER

Jamaica

| 4 small red snappers |
| 2 teaspoons salt |
| 2 fresh red chillies, seeded and finely chopped |
| juice of 2 limes |
| flour for dusting |
| oil for shallow-frying |
| 1 onion, chopped |
| 250g/8oz tomatoes, skinned and chopped |
| 300ml/½ pint water |
| salt and freshly ground black pepper |

To serve:

| lime wedges |
| hot pepper sauce |
| boiled rice |

1 Scale and clean the red snappers. Wash well, inside and out, under running cold water and then pat dry with absorbent kitchen paper. Slash the sides of each fish deeply 2 or 3 times, almost through to the bone.

2 Pound the salt and chopped chilli together in a mortar and sprinkle over the red snappers. Place the fish in a shallow bowl and pour the lime juice over the top. Cover and leave in a cool place for 1-2 hours to marinate.

3 Remove the fish from the bowl, reserving the marinade. Dust them well with flour. Heat the oil in a large frying pan and fry the fish until crisp and golden on both sides, turning once during cooking. Remove and drain on absorbent kitchen paper. Keep warm.

PREPARATION: 10 MINUTES +
MARINATING TIME
COOKING: 35-40 MINUTES
SERVES: 4

4 Pour off most of the oil and fry the onion in the oil left in the pan. When it is soft, add the tomatoes and simmer gently until thickened. Add the water and reserved marinade and bring to the boil. Reduce the heat, add the fried fish and simmer for 5 minutes. Season to taste and serve with lime wedges, hot pepper sauce and rice.

ROLLED STEAK
Cuba

1 Season one side of the steak with salt and pepper, 1 tablespoon of lime juice and the garlic. Arrange the ham strips in a layer over the steak. Soak the carrot in the remaining lime juice for 5 minutes. Drain, discarding the lime juice, and arrange the carrot on top of the ham. Sprinkle with sugar and dot with butter.

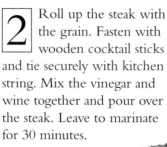

2 Roll up the steak with the grain. Fasten with wooden cocktail sticks and tie securely with kitchen string. Mix the vinegar and wine together and pour over the steak. Leave to marinate for 30 minutes.

1kg/2lb flank steak
salt and freshly ground black pepper
4 tablespoons lime juice
1 garlic clove, crushed
125g/4oz cooked ham, cut into strips
1 carrot, thinly sliced
1 teaspoon sugar
1 tablespoon butter
1 tablespoon red wine vinegar
3 tablespoons dry red wine
3 tablespoons vegetable oil
1 bay leaf
1 onion, thinly sliced
1 green pepper, seeded and chopped
1 tablespoon chopped coriander
500g/1lb tomatoes, skinned and chopped
1 red pepper, seeded and chopped

3 Lift out the steak and pat dry. Reserve the marinade. Heat the oil in a heavy flameproof casserole or saucepan and brown the steak all over. Add the bay leaf, onion, green pepper, coriander, tomatoes, red pepper and the reserved marinade. Cover and simmer for 2 hours, or until the steak is tender.

4 Lift out the steak and remove the string and toothpicks. Slice into serving portions and then arrange on a warmed serving plate. Pour the sauce over the steak and serve.

PREPARATION: 20 MINUTES +
MARINATING TIME
COOKING: 2 HOURS
SERVES: 4-6

PICADILLO
Minced beef stew (Cuba)

1 Heat the oil in a large, deep frying pan and add the onions, garlic and peppers. Fry gently until softened and lightly coloured. Add the chilli and fry for 1 minute. Stir in the minced beef and cook, stirring constantly, until evenly browned.

2 Add the tomatoes, bay leaf, raisins, olives, cumin and vinegar. Simmer gently for 20 minutes until the meat is cooked and the sauce thickens. Stir in the capers and season to taste with salt and pepper. Simmer for 5 more minutes.

3 tablespoons olive oil
2 onions, chopped
3 garlic cloves, crushed
2 green peppers, seeded and chopped
1 fresh red chilli, seeded and finely chopped
675g/1½lb lean minced beef
4 tomatoes, skinned and chopped
1 bay leaf
75g/3oz raisins
75g/3oz pimiento-stuffed green olives, sliced
½ teaspoon ground cumin
1 tablespoon vinegar
3 tablespoons capers
salt and freshly ground black pepper

For the fried plantains:

3-4 ripe black plantains
butter or oil for shallow-frying

PREPARATION: 15 MINUTES
COOKING: 35 MINUTES
SERVES: 4

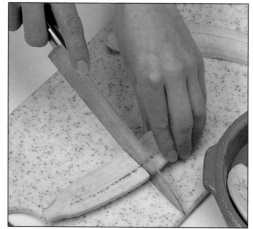

3 While the picadillo is cooking, prepare and fry the plantains. Cut off the ends and peel the plantains. Cut each one in half lengthways and then cut each piece in half again crossways.

4 Heat the butter or oil in a heavy frying pan and add the plantains. Fry gently until they are golden brown on both sides, turning them once. Drain on absorbent kitchen paper and serve with the picadillo.

BEEF AND PINEAPPLE KEBABS
Anguilla

500g/1lb rump steak
3 tomatoes
2 onions
1 green pepper
12 pineapple cubes, fresh or canned
rice, to serve
For the marinade:
1 tablespoon molasses or treacle
4 tablespoons pineapple juice
2 tablespoons vinegar
1 tablespoon oil
salt and freshly ground black pepper

1 Make the marinade: put the molasses or treacle, pineapple juice, vinegar and oil in a bowl and mix well together. Add a little salt and some freshly ground black pepper.

3 Cut the tomatoes into quarters. Peel the onions and cut them into small chunks. Remove the core and seeds from the green pepper, and cut it into squares.

4 Thread the steak, tomatoes, onions, pepper and pineapple chunks alternately on to 4 long or 8 short skewers. Brush them with the reserved marinade. Cook under a hot grill for about 10 minutes, turning frequently and basting often. Serve with plain boiled rice with the remaining marinade poured over the top.

2 Cut the steak into 2.5cm/1 inch cubes and add to the marinade. Cover and leave in a cool place for at least 1 hour. Remove the steak and reserve the marinade for basting the kebabs.

PREPARATION: 20 MINUTES +
MARINATING TIME
COOKING: 10 MINUTES
SERVES: 4

COLOMBO DE PORC

Pork curry (Martinique)

3 tablespoons peanut oil
2 tablespoons butter
1kg/2lb lean pork fillet, cubed
2 onions, finely chopped
2 garlic cloves, crushed
few sprigs of fresh thyme
few sprigs of parsley, chopped
150ml/¼ pint water or stock
1 tablespoon white wine vinegar
1 christophene, peeled and cubed
1 aubergine, peeled and cubed
2 tomatoes, skinned, seeded and chopped

For the Poudre de Colombo:

pinch of turmeric
1 teaspoon ground coriander
2 garlic cloves, crushed
2 fresh red chillies, seeded and finely chopped
2 teaspoons mustard seeds
4 allspice berries
freshly ground black pepper

2 Heat the oil and butter in a deep frying pan or saucepan and add the pork, onions and garlic. Fry over medium heat, stirring frequently, until the pork is browned on all sides and the onions are softened.

4 Add the herbs, water or stock and the vinegar. Cover the pan and cook gently for about 30 minutes. Add the remaining ingredients and continue cooking, uncovered, for about 15 minutes, or until the vegetables are tender and the sauce reduced and thickened. Serve with rice.

3 Add the Poudre de Colombo paste to the pork and onions in the pan and stir well. Cook over gentle heat for about 3 minutes, stirring occasionally.

1 Make the Poudre de Colombo: put the turmeric, coriander, garlic, chillies, mustard seeds, allspice berries and black pepper in a mortar. Mash with a pestle to make a paste.

PREPARATION:
15 MINUTES
COOKING: 1 HOUR
SERVES 4

SPICED PORK ROAST

Jamaica

1 x 2kg/4lb loin of pork joint
125ml/4 fl oz dark rum
600ml/1 pint meat stock
2 teaspoons arrowroot
For the seasoning:
¹/₂ teaspoon ground cloves
¹/₂ teaspoon ground allspice
1 teaspoon ground ginger
2 garlic cloves, crushed
1 bay leaf, crumbled
salt and freshly ground black pepper
For the basting sauce:
75g/3oz soft brown sugar
juice of 1 lime
3 tablespoons rum

1 Mix all the seasoning ingredients together in a small bowl. With a sharp knife, cut through the fat on the pork loin in a diamond pattern. Rub the seasoning over the scored fat.

2 Place the loin of pork in a roasting pan. Pour the rum and 125ml/ 4 fl oz of the stock over the pork. Place in a preheated oven at 180°C/350°F/ Gas Mark 4 and roast for 1³/₄-2 hours.

PREPARATION: 10 MINUTES
COOKING: 2 HOURS
SERVES: 6

3 Mix together the ingredients for the basting sauce and blend well. After 1 hour, remove the pork from the oven and baste with the sauce. Return to the oven for the remainder of the cooking time, adding more stock or a little water if necessary to moisten the meat.

4 When the meat is cooked, transfer it to a serving plate and keep warm. Drain off some of the fat and add the remaining basting sauce and meat stock. Stir well to scrape up any pork residues in the pan. Place over heat and bring to the boil, stirring. Mix the arrowroot with 1 tablespoon of water and stir into the gravy until thickened. Serve with the roast pork.

CHICKEN PILAU

Trinidad

1 Put the seasoning ingredients in a mortar and pound well with a pestle until the garlic and allspice berries are crushed and blended with the salt, pepper and herbs. Rub this mixture all over the chicken pieces and leave in a cool place or the refrigerator for several hours (overnight if wished).

3 Add the onion, garlic, red pepper and chilli to the pan, and fry over gentle heat until softened but not browned. Add the rice to the pan and turn in the oil until all the grains are glistening. Stir in the tomatoes, chicken stock, strands of saffron and thyme.

2 Heat the oil and butter in a large, deep frying pan and add the seasoned chicken pieces. Fry over moderate heat, turning several times, until they are golden brown all over. Remove from the pan and keep warm.

PREPARATION: 10 MINUTES +
MARINATING TIME
COOKING: 40 MINUTES
SERVES: 6

1 x 2kg/4lb chicken, cut into pieces
3 tablespoons groundnut oil
15g/½oz butter
1 onion, finely chopped
2 garlic cloves, crushed
1 red pepper, seeded and chopped
1 red chilli pepper, seeded and finely chopped
375g/12oz long-grain rice
2 tomatoes, skinned and chopped
900ml/1½ pints chicken stock
few strands of saffron
sprig of thyme

For the seasoning:
salt and freshly ground black pepper
1 teaspoon dried mixed herbs
2 allspice berries
1 garlic clove, peeled

For the garnish:
50g/2oz roasted peanuts
chopped fresh red chilli

4 Return the chicken pieces to the pan, cover and simmer for about 20 minutes, or until the rice is tender and has absorbed all the liquid, and the chicken is cooked. Keep checking the pan and stirring the rice to prevent it sticking. Add more liquid if necessary. Serve hot sprinkled with peanuts and chilli.

CHICKEN IN COCONUT MILK

Martinique

3 │ Return the chicken to the pan and pour in the coconut milk. Sprinkle with the strands of saffron and season with salt and pepper. Stir well and simmer for 30-40 minutes, until the chicken is cooked and tender, and the sauce has reduced. Sprinkle with parsley.

1 │ Heat the groundnut oil in a large, deep frying pan and add the chicken quarters. Fry gently over moderate heat until they are golden brown all over. Turn the chicken occasionally in the oil.

3 tablespoons groundnut oil
4 chicken quarters
2 onions, finely chopped
2 garlic cloves, crushed
1 fresh red chilli, finely chopped
450ml/³/4 pint coconut milk
few strands of saffron
salt and pepper
2 tablespoons chopped parsley, to garnish
For the rice:
350g/12oz long-grain rice
1.2 litres/2 pints water
salt

2 │ Remove the chicken and set aside. Add the onions, garlic and chilli to the pan and fry gently for about 5 minutes, until soft. Do not allow the onions to brown – they should be only lightly coloured.

PREPARATION: 10 MINUTES
COOKING: 45-50 MINUTES
SERVES: 4

4 │ Meanwhile, prepare the rice. Wash it thoroughly and drain well. Bring the salted water to the boil and quickly tip in the rice. Simmer vigorously for 15 minutes. Drain and rinse, and then return to the saucepan. Cover and simmer, without water, for 15-20 minutes, until the rice is dry and cooked. Serve with the chicken.

CHICKEN WITH PINEAPPLE

Cuba

1 x 2kg/4lb chicken, cut into 6 pieces

juice of 1 lime

grated zest of 1 lime

salt and freshly ground black pepper

flour for dusting

2 tablespoons olive oil

15g/½oz butter

1 onion, chopped

1 garlic clove, crushed

1 fresh red chilli, seeded and finely chopped

2 tomatoes, skinned and chopped

3 tablespoons raisins

1 teaspoon brown sugar

For the sauce:

1 ripe pineapple, peeled and cored

2 tablespoons rum

3 Add the onion, garlic and chilli, and fry gently for 5 minutes. Add the tomatoes, raisins and brown sugar, mix well and cook gently for a further 10 minutes.

1 Put the chicken pieces in a large bowl. Rub them all over with the lime juice and grated zest, and sprinkle with salt and pepper. Set aside for 30 minutes for the chicken to absorb the flavour of the lime.

PREPARATION: 15 MINUTES +
MARINATING TIME
COOKING: 30 MINUTES
SERVES: 6

2 Dust the chicken pieces lightly with flour. Heat the oil and butter in a large, heavy frying pan. Add the chicken to the hot oil and fry gently over low heat until the chicken is tender and golden brown. Turn the chicken frequently to cook it on both sides.

4 Meanwhile, chop and crush the pineapple, and then mix to a pulp with all its juice in an electric blender. Transfer to a pan and simmer gently until reduced to a quarter of its original volume. Stir in the rum, and then pour the sauce over the chicken and serve.

CHICKEN CALYPSO

Dominica

5 tablespoons groundnut oil
1 x 2kg/4lb chicken, cut into pieces
500g/1lb long-grain rice
1 onion, finely chopped
1 green pepper, seeded and finely chopped
½ teaspoon saffron strands
600ml/1 pint chicken stock
5cm/2-inch piece of lime peel
1 tablespoon rum
dash of Angostura bitters
salt and freshly ground black pepper
125g/4oz mushrooms, sliced

2 Add the rice, onion and green pepper to the pan, and stir well. Fry gently until golden and the rice grains are translucent. Stir in the saffron, chicken stock, lime peel, rum and Angostura bitters.

3 Transfer the rice and vegetable mixture to a heavy flameproof casserole dish, and place the chicken pieces on top. Season well with salt and freshly ground black pepper.

4 Fry the mushrooms in the remaining oil in a clean pan for 5 minutes. Add to the casserole and then cover and simmer gently for about 30 minutes, until the chicken is cooked and all the liquid absorbed. Remove the lid for the last 5 minutes so that the rice is light and fluffy. Serve hot.

1 Heat 3 tablespoons of the oil in a large, heavy frying pan and add the chicken pieces. Fry them until they are golden brown all over, turning them occasionally. Remove the chicken and keep warm.

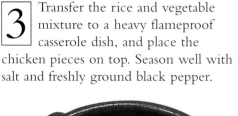

PREPARATION: 10 MINUTES
COOKING: 50 MINUTES
SERVES: 4-6

JAMAICAN JERKED CHICKEN
Jamaica

25g/1oz allspice berries

5cm/2-inch cinnamon stick

1 teaspoon freshly grated nutmeg

1 fresh red chilli, seeded and finely chopped

4 spring onions, thinly sliced

1 bay leaf, crumbled

salt and freshly ground black pepper

1 tablespoon dark rum

6 chicken joints

For the pineapple chutney:

2 fresh pineapples, peeled and chopped

2.5cm/1-inch piece fresh root ginger, peeled and finely chopped

1 onion, finely chopped

1 fresh red chilli, seeded and finely chopped

125ml/4 fl oz vinegar

250g/8oz dark brown sugar

1 Make the jerked seasoning: pound the allspice berries, cinnamon and nutmeg in a mortar, or grind them to a powder in an electric grinder. Add the chilli, spring onions, bay leaf and seasoning to the mortar and continue pounding to a thick paste.

2 Stir the rum into the paste and mix well. Slash the chicken deeply on the skin side 2 or 3 times, and then rub the jerked seasoning paste all over the chicken. Cover and leave in the refrigerator or a cool place for 1-2 hours.

3 Meanwhile, make the pineapple chutney. Put all the ingredients in a saucepan and stir well. Place over moderate heat and stir until the sugar has completely dissolved. Bring to the boil and then reduce the heat a little. Cook vigorously, stirring occasionally, until the chutney thickens.

4 Pour the chutney into sterilized glass jars and seal. If wished, it can be made in advance and kept for 2-3 weeks in a refrigerator. Roast the jerked chicken at 200°C/400°F/Gas Mark 6 for 20-30 minutes, or cook under a hot grill. Serve with the pineapple chutney and plain boiled rice.

PREPARATION: 20 MINUTES +
MARINATING TIME
COOKING: 20-30 MINUTES
SERVES: 6

GRILLED CHICKEN CREOLE

St Lucia

1 Prepare the seasoning: put the spring onions, onion, garlic, chilli, herbs and allspice berries in a bowl. Add the lime juice and olive oil and stir well to mix thoroughly together.

2 Slash the chicken breasts 2 or 3 times on both sides, and season lightly with salt and pepper. Rub the seasoning over both sides of each chicken breast, pressing it into the slashes. Cover and chill in the refrigerator for 2–3 hours.

4 While the chicken is cooking, make the avocado sauce. Mash the avocado to a smooth paste and beat in the onion, garlic and a little cayenne pepper. Add a little lime juice, if wished. This will prevent the sauce discolouring. Serve with the grilled chicken, with some rice.

6 chicken breasts, skinned and boned
salt and freshly ground black pepper

For the seasoning:
2 spring onions, finely chopped
1/2 red onion, finely chopped
2 garlic cloves, crushed
1 fresh red chilli, seeded and finely chopped
3 chives, snipped
few sprigs of thyme, chopped
few sprigs of parsley, chopped
3 allspice berries, crushed
juice of 1 lime
2 tablespoons olive oil

For the avocado sauce:
1 large ripe avocado
1 tablespoon finely chopped onion
1/2 garlic clove, crushed
cayenne pepper, to taste
lime juice (optional)

3 Put the chicken breasts on a grill pan and cook under a hot grill, turning once, until cooked on both sides. Take care that the herbs do not burn. Alternatively, cook them in a preheated oven at 200°C/400°F/Gas Mark 6 for about 20 minutes.

PREPARATION: 10 MINUTES +
MARINATING TIME
COOKING: 15-20 MINUTES
SERVES: 4

CHICKEN CURRY
Guadeloupe

1 Heat the oil in a heavy frying pan and add the chicken pieces. Fry over moderate heat until golden brown all over, turning several times to cook both sides. Remove from the pan and place in a flameproof casserole dish.

2 Add the onions, garlic and chilli to the frying pan and cook, stirring occasionally, over medium heat until the onions are softened and golden, about 5 minutes.

3 Add the curry powder to the onion mixture and stir well. Continue cooking for 3 minutes, stirring. Add the aubergine, christophene, papaya and tomatoes, and cook for 2–3 minutes.

| 5 tablespoons groundnut oil |
| 1 x 2kg/4lb chicken, cut into 6 or 8 serving pieces |
| 2 onions, finely chopped |
| 1 garlic clove, crushed |
| 1 fresh red chilli, seeded and finely chopped |
| 2 tablespoons curry powder |
| 250g/8oz aubergine, peeled and cubed |
| 1 christophene, peeled and cubed |
| 1 unripe green papaya, peeled and sliced |
| 2 tomatoes, skinned and chopped |
| 150ml/¼ pint chicken stock |
| 150ml/¼ pint coconut milk |
| 2 tablespoons lime juice |
| salt and freshly ground black pepper |
| 1 tablespoon rum or Madeira |
| rice and fried bananas, to serve |

4 Put the curried mixture into the casserole with the chicken and add the chicken stock and coconut milk. Cover and simmer for about 30 minutes, until the chicken is cooked and the vegetables are tender. Stir in the lime juice, seasoning and rum. Serve with plain boiled rice and fried bananas.

PREPARATION: 10 MINUTES
COOKING: 50 MINUTES
SERVES: 4-6

COO-COO

Barbados

1 Wash the okra and cut off the stems. Cut them into 5mm/¼-inch thick slices. Bring the water to the boil in a large saucepan and add the prepared okra and the salt. Boil until tender.

2 Slowly add the cornmeal to the saucepan in a thin stream, stirring all the time with a wooden spoon. Keep stirring to prevent any lumps forming and removing any cornmeal from the sides of the pan.

3 Add the sugar and continue cooking over moderate heat for about 5-10 minutes, stirring all the time. When cooked, the coo-coo mixture will be thick and smooth.

12 okra
1.5 litres/2½ pints water
good pinch of salt
250g/8oz yellow cornmeal
1 tablespoon sugar
25g/1oz butter
To serve:
cooked sweet potatoes
sliced tomatoes
sliced pimentos

4 Place the butter in a warmed round bowl or basin and add the coo-coo. Roll it around in the bowl until it forms a ball. Serve, cut into slices, with sweet potatoes, tomatoes and pimentos.

PREPARATION: 10 MINUTES
COOKING: 20-25 MINUTES
SERVES: 6

PUMPKIN CURRY

St Lucia

1 Put the grated fresh coconut in a bowl and add the coconut water. You can drain this out of a fresh coçonut by piercing it a couple of times with a skewer and draining out the liquid. Leave the coconut to soak for about 30 minutes.

4 Add the pumpkin, tomatoes and the coconut and coconut water. Bring to the boil and then reduce the heat to a bare simmer. Cover the pan and cook gently for 15-20 minutes, until the pumpkin is tender but not mushy. Season to taste with salt and pepper and serve hot.

2 Heat the vegetable oil in a large, heavy saucepan and add the onion, green pepper and garlic. Fry gently over very low heat, stirring occasionally, until the onion and pepper are softened and golden brown.

3 Add the fresh root ginger, turmeric, chillies and cloves to the onion and pepper mixture. Stir well and continue cooking over low heat for 2-3 minutes, stirring.

125g/4oz fresh coconut, grated
300ml/½ pint coconut water (from a fresh coconut)
2 tablespoons vegetable oil
1 onion, chopped
1 green pepper, seeded and chopped
4 garlic cloves, crushed
2 slices fresh root ginger, peeled and finely chopped
1 tablespoon turmeric
2 fresh green chillies, seeded and finely chopped
¼ teaspoon ground cloves
750g/1½lb pumpkin, peeled, seeded and cut into 2.5cm/1-inch cubes
2 tomatoes, skinned and chopped
salt and freshly ground black pepper

PREPARATION: 20 MINUTES +
SOAKING TIME
COOKING: 30-35 MINUTES
SERVES: 4-6

CHRISTOPHENE AU GRATIN

Guadeloupe

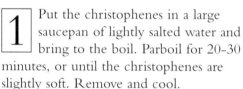

2-3 large christophenes
50g/2oz butter
1 onion, finely chopped
salt and freshly ground black pepper
125g/4oz grated cheese, e.g. Cheddar
25g/1oz dry breadcrumbs

1 Put the christophenes in a large saucepan of lightly salted water and bring to the boil. Parboil for 20-30 minutes, or until the christophenes are slightly soft. Remove and cool.

3 Heat the butter in a small frying pan and add the onion. Cook until soft and transparent. Season to taste with salt and pepper and stir in the christophene pulp. Cook gently over low heat for 2 minutes. Stir in half of the grated cheese.

4 Pile the christophene and onion mixture into the reserved shells and top with the remaining cheese and breadcrumbs. Place on a baking sheet and cook in a preheated oven at 180°C/350°F/Gas Mark 4 for 15-20 minutes, until delicately browned.

2 Cut each christophene in half lengthways and carefully scoop out the pulp, leaving the shells intact. Chop and mash the pulp, and reserve the shells.

PREPARATION: 10 MINUTES
COOKING: 35-50 MINUTES
SERVES: 4-6

FRIJOLES NEGROS

Black beans (Cuba)

1 Wash the black beans thoroughly under running cold water and then drain them. Put them in a large, heavy-based saucepan with the water and bring to the boil.

2 Reduce the heat to a bare simmer, cover the saucepan and cook very gently for about 1¹/₂-2 hours, until the beans are tender but not mushy. Keep checking the beans and adding more liquid if necessary.

PREPARATION: 15 MINUTES
COOKING: 2-2¹/₂ HOURS
SERVES: 6

3 While the beans are cooking, heat the oil in a frying pan and add the salt pork or ham. Sauté gently for 2-3 minutes and then add the onion, garlic, green pepper and chilli. Cook, stirring occasionally, until the vegetables are softened.

4 Add the onion mixture to the pan of beans, together with the bay leaf and a little salt and pepper. Simmer gently for 30 minutes. Remove a ladleful of beans and mash well. Return to the pan and stir well. The consistency of the sauce should be thick but not too liquid. Serve hot, garnished with chopped spring onions.

500g/1lb dried black beans
750ml/1¹/₄ pints water
2 tablespoons vegetable oil
50g/2oz salt pork or ham hock, chopped
1 onion, finely chopped
1 garlic clove, crushed
1 green pepper, seeded and chopped
1 fresh green chilli, seeded and finely chopped
1 bay leaf
salt and freshly ground black pepper
2 spring onions, chopped, to garnish

OKRA CREOLE-STYLE

St Lucia

1 Prepare the okra: wash it well and dry on absorbent kitchen paper. Cut off the stems with a sharp knife and then slice the okra into 5mm/¼-inch rounds. Set aside.

3 Add the tomatoes and fresh corn kernels and stir well. Season with salt and pepper to taste, and then add the lime juice. Reduce the heat and cook gently over low heat for 15–20 minutes, until the okra are tender and the sauce is reduced and thickened.

12–16 okra
3 tablespoons groundnut oil
1 large onion, thinly sliced
1 green pepper, seeded and chopped
2 garlic cloves, crushed
500g/1lb tomatoes, skinned and chopped
250g/8oz fresh corn kernels
salt and freshly ground black pepper
juice of ½ lime
dash of hot pepper sauce
fresh coriander, to garnish

2 Heat the groundnut oil in a large, heavy frying pan and add the onion, green pepper and garlic. Fry gently over medium heat until slightly browned, stirring occasionally. Add the okra and continue cooking for 5 minutes.

4 While the okra are cooking, stir occasionally to stop the sauce sticking to the base of the pan. Just before serving, add a dash of hot pepper sauce. Transfer to a serving dish and garnish with coriander.

PREPARATION: 10 MINUTES
COOKING: 25–30 MINUTES
SERVES: 4–6

BANANA CURRY

Bermuda

1 Melt the butter in a large, heavy-based saucepan. Add the onions and fry gently over very low heat until softened and translucent. Take care that they do not brown.

2 Meanwhile, soak the sultanas in a little boiling water for 2-3 minutes to plump them up. Drain and add to the onions with the apple and salt. Stir in the flour and curry powder and cook, stirring constantly, for 3-4 minutes.

3 Remove the saucepan from the heat and gradually stir in the coconut milk and water, a little at a time. Return to the heat and cook very gently, stirring until thickened.

50g/2oz butter
2 small onions, chopped
75g/3oz sultanas
1 dessert apple, peeled, cored and diced
$^1/_2$ teaspoon salt
40g/1$^1/_2$oz flour
2 teaspoons curry powder
300ml/$^1/_2$ pint coconut milk
300ml/$^1/_2$ pint water
4 under-ripe green bananas, peeled and diagonally sliced
4 hard-boiled eggs, quartered
mango chutney and boiled rice, to serve

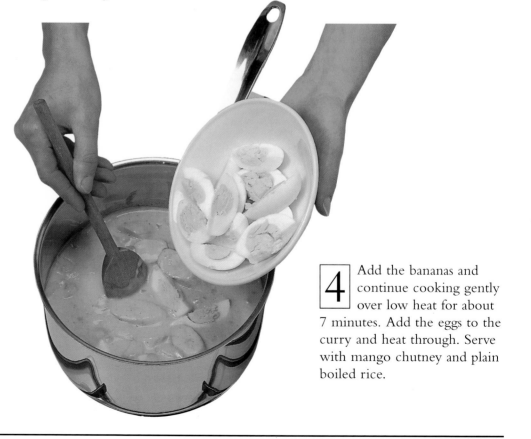

4 Add the bananas and continue cooking gently over low heat for about 7 minutes. Add the eggs to the curry and heat through. Serve with mango chutney and plain boiled rice.

PREPARATION: 10 MINUTES
COOKING: 20-25 MINUTES
SERVES: 4

ORANGE-BAKED SWEET POTATOES

Bahamas

4-5 sweet potatoes

5 large oranges

4 tablespoons cream

25g/1oz butter

1 tablespoon sugar

1 tablespoon dark rum

salt and freshly grated black pepper

pinch of ground cinnamon

2 Slice the tops off 4 of the oranges and scoop out the flesh without breaking the shells. Cut the peel from the tops into thin strips for the garnish. Squeeze the juice from the pulp and grate the rind from the fifth orange.

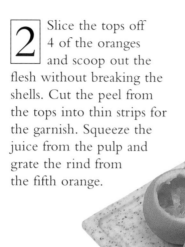

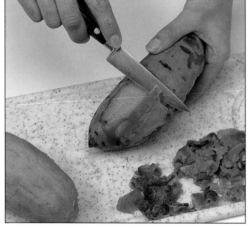

1 Wash the potatoes and place in a saucepan of lightly salted water. Bring to the boil and then continue boiling for about 30 minutes, until the potatoes are tender. Drain and peel them, and then set aside.

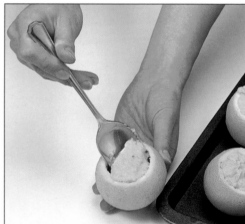

3 Put the peeled sweet potatoes in a bowl and mash thoroughly. Add the cream, butter, sugar and rum and mix well together, beating until blended. Add 4 tablespoons of the squeezed orange juice and the grated rind. Season with salt and pepper and the cinnamon.

4 Spoon the mashed potato mixture into the 4 orange shells. Place on a baking tray and bake in a preheated oven at 180°C/350°F/Gas Mark 4 for 15-20 minutes, until golden brown on top. Garnish with the reserved strips of orange peel and serve.

PREPARATION: 10 MINUTES
COOKING: 50 MINUTES
SERVES: 4

RICE AND PEAS

Jamaica

1 Put the dried red kidney beans in a large bowl and cover with cold water. Leave to soak overnight. The following day, rinse the kidney beans and drain well.

2 Put the kidney beans in a large saucepan and add 900ml/1½ pints boiling water. Cook for about 30 minutes, until the kidney beans are almost tender.

3 Add the coconut milk, thyme, spring onions and chilli to the saucepan. Season with salt and pepper and bring back to boiling point. Boil rapidly for 5 minutes.

4 Add the rice and stir well. Cover and simmer gently over very low heat until the rice is tender and all the liquid has been absorbed. This will take about 20-25 minutes. If there is any remaining liquid, drain the rice and 'peas' (kidney beans). Transfer to a serving dish and serve hot.

250g/8oz dried red kidney beans
600ml/1 pint coconut milk
2 sprigs of fresh thyme
2 spring onions, finely chopped
1 fresh green chilli, seeded and finely chopped
salt and freshly ground black pepper
500g/1lb long-grain rice

PREPARATION: 5 MINUTES +
SOAKING TIME
COOKING: 55 MINUTES
SERVES: 6

STUFFED GREEN PEPPERS

Trinidad

1 Place the peppers in a large saucepan and cover with cold water. Bring to the boil, then reduce the heat and simmer gently until the peppers are tender but still firm. Drain and allow to cool.

2 Prepare the stuffing: heat the oil in a large frying pan and add the onion, garlic and chilli. Fry gently over low heat until the onion is softened and golden brown.

3 Add the minced beef and stir well. Continue cooking over low heat until well browned. Add the lemon rind and cooked rice. Season with salt and pepper and paprika. Cook gently for 5 minutes and then stir in the chives.

| 4 large green peppers |
| 2 tablespoons vegetable oil |
| 1 small onion, finely chopped |
| 1 garlic clove, crushed |
| 1 fresh red chilli, seeded and finely chopped |
| 125g/4oz minced beef |
| grated rind of 1 lemon |
| 4 tablespoons cooked rice |
| salt and freshly ground black pepper |
| pinch of paprika |
| few chives, chopped |
| 4 tomatoes, thinly sliced |
| snipped chives, to garnish |

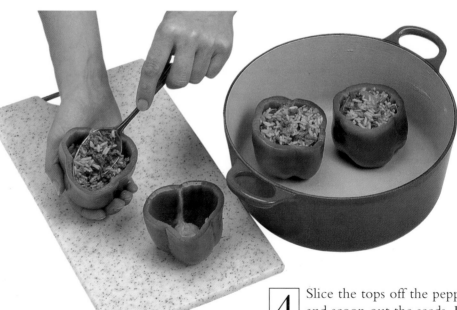

4 Slice the tops off the peppers and scoop out the seeds. Fill with the stuffing and stand in a greased baking tin. Surround with the tomatoes and bake in a preheated oven at 180°C/350°F/Gas Mark 4 for about 20 minutes. Sprinkle with chives.

PREPARATION: 15 MINUTES
COOKING: 45 MINUTES
SERVES: 4

RUM PANCAKES
Barbados

1 Sift the flour into a bowl and make a well in the centre. Stir in the sugar, eggs, olive oil and rum. Blend thoroughly, drawing in the flour from the sides, until the mixture is smooth.

2 Gradually add the milk, a little at a time, beating well between each addition. The batter should be smooth and the consistency of single cream. Add a little more milk if necessary and then leave to stand for 1 hour.

3 Brush a small omelette pan with a little oil and heat thoroughly. Pour in sufficient batter to cover the base of the pan thinly, tilting the pan until evenly covered. Cook until the underside of the batter is set and golden brown, and then flip the pancake over and cook the other side. Remove and keep warm. Cook the remaining pancakes in the same way.

4 Make the filling: whip the cream until thick and gently stir in the rum and sugar. Spread the warm pancakes with the filling and roll up or fold over. Sprinkle with grated chocolate and serve the pancakes immediately.

150g/5oz plain flour
1 teaspoon sugar
2 eggs
1 tablespoon olive oil
1 tablespoon rum
300ml/½ pint milk
oil for frying
grated chocolate, to decorate
For the filling:
300ml/½ pint double cream
2 tablespoons rum
2 teaspoons caster sugar

PREPARATION: 10 MINUTES +
STANDING TIME
COOKING: 10 MINUTES
SERVES: 4-6

STUFFED BANANAS

Haiti

1 Put the raisins in a small bowl with 2 tablespoons of the rum and set aside while you prepare the dessert. The raisins plump up in the rum and are used for decoration.

2 Peel the bananas and then cut each one in half lengthways, and then in half crossways. Place them in a bowl and sprinkle with the lime juice to prevent discolouration. Set aside.

3 In a bowl, cream the butter and sugar together until the mixture is smooth and creamy. Add the remaining rum, and beat thoroughly. Fold the cashew nuts into the butter mixture.

| 2 tablespoons seedless raisins |
| 4 tablespoons dark rum |
| 3 large, ripe bananas |
| 4 tablespoons lime juice |
| 125g/4oz butter |
| 50g/2oz icing sugar |
| 3 tablespoons chopped toasted cashew nuts |

4 Carefully scoop out a cavity, about 1.25cm/½ inch deep, in each banana and stuff with the nut and butter mixture. Decorate with the raisins and pour over any rum that has not been absorbed. Chill thoroughly for 2–3 hours before serving.

PREPARATION: 15 MINUTES +
CHILLING TIME
SERVES: 3-6

CLAFOUTIS AUX FRUITS EXOTIQUES
Exotic fruit batter pudding (Guadeloupe)

1 Cut the fresh pineapple and mango flesh into 1.25cm/½-inch chunks. Put the prepared fruit in a bowl and sprinkle with the rum. Set aside while you make the batter.

4 Arrange the pineapple and mango in a buttered shallow, ovenproof dish. Pour the batter mixture over them and bake in a preheated oven at 200°C/400°F/Gas Mark 6 for 25–30 minutes, until risen and set. Cool a little and serve lukewarm, sprinkled with caster sugar.

2 Break the eggs into a bowl and beat lightly together. Sift the flour and salt and blend well with the beaten eggs. Whisk in the sugar until the mixture is smooth.

3 Heat the milk with the vanilla pod but do not allow to boil. Remove from the heat and allow to infuse for 5 minutes. Remove the vanilla pod and strain the milk into the egg mixture, a little at a time, beating well until thoroughly blended. Beat in the rum from the soaked fruit.

500g/1lb fresh pineapple and mango, peeled
2 tablespoons dark rum
3 eggs
20g/¾oz plain flour
pinch of salt
50g/2oz caster sugar
300ml/½ pint milk
1 vanilla pod
butter for greasing
caster sugar for sprinkling

PREPARATION: 15 MINUTES
COOKING: 25–30 MINUTES
SERVES: 4–6

BANANA BREAD

St Lucia

1 Put the butter and sugar in a large mixing bowl and beat together until light and creamy. Beat in the eggs, one at a time, and then stir in the rum (if using).

2 Sift all the dry ingredients – the self-raising flour, salt, bicarbonate of soda, grated nutmeg and cinnamon – into another clean bowl and set aside.

PREPARATION: 15 MINUTES
COOKING: 1 HOUR
MAKES: 1 LOAF

3 Peel the bananas and using a fork mash them with the vanilla essence. Gradually add the flour mixture and the banana mixture to the creamed egg, butter and sugar, beating thoroughly after each addition. Toss the raisins and walnuts in a little flour and then fold into the banana mixture.

125g/4oz butter, softened
175g/6oz caster sugar
2 eggs
2 tablespoons rum (optional)
250g/8oz self-raising flour
½ teaspoon salt
¼ teaspoon bicarbonate of soda
1 teaspoon grated nutmeg
½ teaspoon ground cinnamon
2-3 large, ripe bananas
1 teaspoon vanilla essence
75g/3oz seedless raisins
75g/3oz chopped walnuts

4 Pour the mixture into a greased 23 x 13cm/9 x 5-inch loaf tin. Bake in a preheated oven at 180°C/350°F/Gas Mark 4 for 1 hour, or until a skewer inserted into the centre of the bread comes out clean. Turn out and cool on a wire rack. Serve sliced, with or without butter. In the Caribbean, this is served as a dessert or may be offered for breakfast.

LIME MERINGUE PIE
Virgin Islands

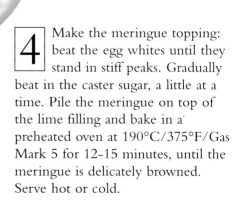

1 Make the pie filling: put the grated lime rind and juice in a heavy-based saucepan with the caster sugar and eggs. Place over very low heat and stir well.

2 Cut the butter into small dice and add to the lime mixture in the pan, one cube at a time. Continue stirring all the time over low heat, until all the butter has been incorporated and the mixture is hot.

3 Pour the lime mixture into the prepared pastry case and place in the centre of a preheated oven at 190°C/375°F/Gas Mark 5 for about 10 minutes, or until the filling is just set. Remove from the oven and cool.

1 x 23cm/9-inch baked pastry case
For the filling:
grated rind and juice of 3 limes
175g/6oz caster sugar
3 eggs, beaten
250g/8oz butter
For the meringue:
3 egg whites
75g/3oz caster sugar

PREPARATION: 15 MINUTES
COOKING: 35 MINUTES
SERVES: 6-8

4 Make the meringue topping: beat the egg whites until they stand in stiff peaks. Gradually beat in the caster sugar, a little at a time. Pile the meringue on top of the lime filling and bake in a preheated oven at 190°C/375°F/Gas Mark 5 for 12-15 minutes, until the meringue is delicately browned. Serve hot or cold.

BANANA RUM FRITTERS
Martinique

| 4 large, ripe bananas |
| 25g/1oz sugar |
| 5 tablespoons dark rum |
| oil for deep-frying |
| **For the batter:** |
| 75g/3oz plain flour |
| pinch of salt |
| 1 tablespoon olive oil |
| 150ml/¼ pint water |
| 2 egg whites |
| **To serve:** |
| vanilla sugar |
| ground cinnamon |

1 Peel the bananas and then cut them diagonally into slices, about 1.25cm/½-inch thick. Place them in a shallow dish and sprinkle with sugar. Pour the rum over the top and set aside for 1½ hours, turning from time to time.

2 Meanwhile, make the batter: sift the flour and salt together into a bowl. Make a well in the centre and gradually mix in the oil and water. Mix to a smooth batter and leave to stand for 1 hour.

3 Just before the batter is needed, beat the egg whites stiffly and then lightly fold them into the batter. Drain the banana slices and dip them into the batter so that they are completely coated.

PREPARATION: 15 MINUTES +
STANDING TIME
COOKING: 10 MINUTES
SERVES: 4

4 Heat the oil for deep-frying and when it is very hot (190°C/375°F), fry the banana pieces, a few at a time, until golden brown on both sides. Drain on absorbent kitchen paper. Serve the fritters really hot, sprinkled with vanilla sugar and cinnamon.

AVOCADO ICE CREAM

Jamaica

1 Break the eggs into a large mixing bowl and beat lightly together. Add 50g/2oz of the sugar and beat lightly. Heat the milk in a saucepan until very hot but do not allow it to boil.

2 Pour the hot milk into the egg mixture, stirring well to mix it thoroughly. Pour the milk and egg mixture into the top of a double boiler and stir over hot simmering water until the custard thickens and coats the back of a spoon. Alternatively, place the basin over a pan of simmering water and stir until thick. Stir in the vanilla or almond essence and set aside to cool.

3 Cut the avocados in half and remove the peel and stones. Mash them in a bowl with the remaining sugar and lime juice. Beat well.

4 eggs
125g/4oz sugar
600ml/1 pint milk
1/2 teaspoon vanilla or almond essence
2 medium-sized ripe avocado pears
good squeeze of lime juice

4 Mix the custard into the mashed avocado and turn into a freezer tray. Freeze lightly until the mixture is slushy. Remove from the refrigerator, beat again and then return to the freezer until frozen.

PREPARATION: 20 MINUTES +
FREEZING TIME
SERVES: 6-8

MANGO FOOL

Jamaica

1 Peel the mangoes and cut out the stones. Chop the flesh into small pieces and place in a saucepan with the sugar, lime juice and water. Simmer gently over low heat until soft and pulpy.

2 Push the mango mixture through a sieve, and then beat the purée thoroughly until smooth. Cover and set aside to cool while you make the custard.

PREPARATION: 15 MINUTES + CHILLING TIME
COOKING: 15-20 MINUTES
SERVES: 4-6

3 Break the egg into a bowl and beat lightly. Heat the milk to scalding point and then stir into the beaten egg. Return to the heat and stir constantly over very low heat until the custard thickens. Do not allow to boil.

4 Remove the custard from the heat and allow to cool. Stir in the mango purée and the cream. Do not blend thoroughly; the fool should look streaky. Pour into glasses or individual dishes and chill before serving.

6 mangoes
125g/4oz sugar
juice of 1/2 lime
150ml/1/4 pint water
1 egg
150ml/1/4 pint milk
125ml/4 fl oz double cream

SAUCES, DRINKS AND CHUTNEYS

RUM PUNCH

1 part fresh lime juice
2 parts sugar
3 parts dark rum
4 parts crushed ice
dash of Angostura bitters
grated nutmeg
To decorate:
sprig of mint or lime leaf
sliced pineapple or orange

Put the lime juice, sugar, rum, ice and bitters in a cocktail shaker, and shake together vigorously. Pour into a glass and serve with grated nutmeg, decorated with a sprig of mint or a lime leaf, and fresh pineapple or orange slices.

WEST INDIES CHUTNEY

1kg/2lb cooking apples, peeled, cored and chopped
1 large onion, finely chopped
125g/4oz soft brown sugar
1 teaspoon salt
1/2 tablespoon mixed pickling spice
1/2 teaspoon ground ginger
300ml/1/2 pint vinegar
175g/6oz treacle

Put all the ingredients in a heavy preserving pan and stir thoroughly. Bring to the boil, stirring all the time. Reduce the heat and simmer, uncovered, for 2 hours, until the chutney is thick and jammy. Allow to cool a little before bottling in sterilized jars. Store in a cool, dark place. Serve with grilled meat, chicken and curries. Makes 2-3 jars.

BARBECUE SAUCE

2 large onions, chopped
4 garlic cloves, crushed
2 tablespoons tomato purée
2 teaspoons cayenne pepper
4 tablespoons lime juice
4 tablespoons olive oil
2 celery sticks, chopped
2 tablespoons brown sugar
2 sprigs of thyme
4 chillies, chopped
1 tablespoon salt
4 bay leaves

Mix the onion, garlic, tomato purée, cayenne pepper and lime juice. Heat the oil in a saucepan and add the onion mixture. Cook very gently for 10 minutes, and then add the remaining ingredients. Bring to the boil and then simmer gently for 30 minutes. Serve with grilled meat, chicken or fish. Serves 4-6.

CREOLE PEPPER SAUCE

1 onion, finely chopped
1 green pepper, seeded and chopped
1 red pepper, seeded and chopped
2 garlic cloves, crushed
4 tablespoons oil
2 tomatoes, skinned and chopped
150ml/1/4 pint chicken stock
150ml/1/4 pint dry white wine
salt and freshly ground black pepper
juice of 1/2 lime
2 teaspoons vinegar
dash of hot pepper sauce

Fry the onion, peppers and garlic in the oil until softened. Add the tomatoes, stir well and cook for 2-3 minutes. Add the stock and wine and cook over medium heat for about 15 minutes, until thickened, stirring occasionally. Season to taste with salt and pepper, and add the lime juice, vinegar and a dash of hot pepper sauce. Serve with fish, meat or chicken. Serves 4-6.

AVOCADO SAUCE

1 large ripe avocado
1 tablespoon finely chopped onion
1 garlic clove, crushed
cayenne pepper, to taste

Halve, stone and peel the avocado, and mash the flesh to a smooth paste. Beat in the onion and garlic and season with cayenne pepper. Serve immediately with chicken, fish and rice dishes. The sauce cannot be prepared in advance as it will discolour if left standing for any length of time, although adding a little lemon juice will help retain the pale green colour. Serves 4.

PEANUT SAUCE

2 tablespoons grated onion
2 tablespoons olive oil
2 tablespoons dark brown sugar
1 teaspoon lime juice
2 tablespoons peanut butter
6 tablespoons coconut cream
pinch of salt

Fry the onion gently in the oil until softened, and then stir in the brown sugar, lime juice and peanut butter. Add the coconut cream, a little at a time,